10/09 Direct

Dust Storms

By Jim Mezzanotte

Science and curriculum consultant: Debra Voege, M.A.,
science and math curriculum resource teacher

Reading specialist: Linda Cornwell, Literacy Connections Consulting

WEEKLY READER®
PUBLISHING

Please visit our web site at **www.garethstevens.com**.
For a free color catalog describing our list of high-quality books,
call 1-800-542-2595 (USA) or 1-800-387-3178 (Canada).
Our fax: 1-877-542-2596

Library of Congress Cataloging-in-Publication Data

Mezzanotte, Jim.
    Dust storms / by Jim Mezzanotte ; science and curriculum consultant, Debra Voege.
        p. cm. — (Wild weather)
    Includes bibliographical references and index.
    ISBN-10: 1-4339-2346-7   ISBN-13: 978-1-4339-2346-3 (lib. bdg.)
    ISBN-10: 1-4339-2360-2   ISBN-13: 978-1-4339-2360-9 (soft cover)
    1. Dust storms—Juvenile literature. I. Title.
QC958.M493   2010
551.55'9—dc22   2009001942

This edition first published in 2010 by
Weekly Reader® Books
An Imprint of Gareth Stevens Publishing
1 Reader's Digest Road
Pleasantville, NY 10570-7000 USA

Executive Managing Editor: Lisa M. Herrington
Senior Editor: Barbara Bakowski
Creative Director: Lisa Donovan
Designer: Melissa Welch, *Studio Montage*
Photo Researcher: Diane Laska-Swanke

Photo credits: Cover, title, pp. 5, 7, 15, 16, 17 © AP Images; pp. 3, 4, 10, 14, 20, 22, 24 © PhotoDisc/
Elements; p. 6 © Dr. Marli Miller/Visuals Unlimited; p. 8 © Jane Thomas/Visuals Unlimited; p. 9 Kami
Strunsee/© Gareth Stevens, Inc.; p. 11 Scott M. Krall/© Gareth Stevens, Inc.; p. 12 © NASA/Goddard
Space Flight Center Scientific Visualization Studio; p. 13 © Mark Atkins/Shutterstock; p. 18 © NOAA;
p. 19 © Oralleff/Shutterstock; p. 21 © Rodolfo Arpia/Shutterstock

Printed in the United States of America

1 2 3 4 5 6 7 8 9 12 11 10 09

Table of Contents

Words in **boldface** are defined in the glossary.

CHAPTER 1
Here Comes a Dust Storm!

In a dust storm, strong winds blow big clouds of dust. The winds blow across the ground. They lift up sand or tiny pieces of rock and dirt.

A large dust storm rolls over Phoenix, Arizona.

A dust cloud can be thousands of feet tall. It moves quickly across the ground. Dust fills the air and blocks out sunlight.

This sandy desert in California is called Death Valley. It is the hottest and driest place in North America.

Dust storms mostly happen in **deserts.** A desert is a place that gets little rain. The ground is dry and often sandy. Wind blows the sand, making dust storms.

Sometimes, dust storms happen after a **drought.** A drought is a long time when no rain falls. The ground turns dry, and plants die.

A farmer in China walks through a field of dying plants. Droughts harm soil, people, and animals.

The Sahara gets many dust storms. That desert is in northern Africa. It is the largest desert in the world.

China, Australia, and countries in the Middle East have dust storms, too. The United States gets a few dust storms in the Southwest.

This map shows the world's largest deserts. Dust from some deserts blows across the ocean.

NORTH AMERICA

United States

Pacific Ocean

Atlantic Ocean

EUROPE

ASIA

Middle East

China

Pacific Ocean

Sahara Desert

AFRICA

SOUTH AMERICA

Indian Ocean

AUSTRALIA

N
W   E
S

= desert

CHAPTER 2
Dust Storms in Action

How do dust storms start? The Sun warms air that is near the ground. The warm air rises, causing winds that lift up the dust.

Thunderstorms can bring dust storms in deserts. Cold winds blow down from the clouds and pick up sand. This kind of dust storm is called a **haboob.**

thundercloud

cold winds

dust storm

A dust storm may begin with a thundercloud's cold winds. Those winds kick up dust and push the storm forward.

This photo was taken from space. The red areas show dust blowing across the Pacific Ocean.

Dust can travel hundreds of miles! Dust from Asia sometimes blows across the ocean to the United States.

Sometimes, dust in the air mixes with raindrops. Then "mud rain" falls. Tiny drops of mud hit the ground.

CHAPTER 3

Dangerous Dust Storms

A dust storm can cause many problems.
Dust gets inside houses, even if the
doors and windows are closed.
Dust gets into machines and makes
them break down.

When people are outdoors, blowing dust stings their skin. It blows into their eyes, noses, and mouths, too. They have to cover their faces.

People who live with dust storms must cover their faces. This woman puts a mask on her dog to protect it from the dust, too.

A dust storm, like this one in Oklahoma, can bury roads. People cannot see to drive. Airports and schools may close.

Dust storms can be bad for farmers.
Strong winds blow away **topsoil.** Topsoil
is the dirt on the surface of the ground.
Plants need rich topsoil to grow.

Farmers plant trees on a hillside in
China. Trees block wind and help
stop soil from blowing away.

A dust storm blows through Texas in April 1935.

In the 1930s, a drought hit the middle of the United States. Winds blew away the topsoil. Farmers could not grow **crops.** The area became known as the **Dust Bowl.**

Cars and factories make smoke and other **pollution.** When a dust storm happens, pollution in the air mixes with dust. It may be carried to places that are far away.

CHAPTER 4
Staying Safe in Dust Storms

Scientists study dust storms. They use
a special tool to measure wind speed.
They warn people who may be
in danger.

This weather tool measures the wind speed near Los Angeles, California.

During a dust storm, the safest place is inside a house. People in cars should pull over to the side of the road. They should keep the car lights turned on.

Glossary

crops: plants that farmers grow for food

deserts: places that get little rain and have dry, sandy soil

drought: a time when little or no rain falls

Dust Bowl: central part of the United States that was hit by dust storms in the 1930s

haboob: a dust storm with very strong winds, occurring mostly in northern Africa, India, and the U.S. Southwest

pollution: waste created by people that is harmful to living things

topsoil: a layer of dirt on the surface of the ground that is good for growing crops

For More Information

Books

Droughts. Weather Update (series). Nathan Olson (Capstone, 2006)

Life in the Dust Bowl. Picture the Past (series). Sally Senzell Isaacs (Heinemann, 2002)

Web Sites

National Drought Mitigation Center: Drought for Kids
www.drought.unl.edu/kids/index.htm
Find facts, photos, maps, and a glossary.

Science News for Kids: A Dire Shortage of Water
www.sciencenewsforkids.org/articles/ 20040825/Feature1.asp
Find information, links, and a word find.

Publisher's note to educators and parents: Our editors have carefully reviewed these web sites to ensure that they are suitable for children. Many web sites change frequently, however, and we cannot guarantee that a site's future contents will continue to meet our high standards of quality and educational value. Be advised that children should be closely supervised whenever they access the Internet.

Index

About the Author

Jim Mezzanotte has written many books for children. He lives in Milwaukee, Wisconsin, with his wife and two sons. He has always been interested in weather, especially big storms.